D0235834

CLASS 746.6

AUTHOR. WILLIAMS, M.

449965

START-A-CRAFT
Fabric Painting

Get started in a new craft with easy-to-follow

projects for beginners

MELANIE WILLIAMS

THE
APPLE
PRESS

A QUINTET BOOK

Published by The Apple Press
6 Blundell Street.
London N7 9BH

Copyright © 1994 Quintet Publishing
Limited. All rights reserved. No part of this
publication may be reproduced. stored in a
retrieval system or transmitted in any form or
by any means. electronic. mechanical.
photocopying. recording or otherwise.
without the permission of the copyright
holder.

ISBN 1−85076−503−0

This book was designed and produced by
Quintet Publishing Limited
6 Blundell Street
London N7 9BH

Creative Director: Richard Dewing
Designers: Ian Hunt and Linda Henley
Senior Editor: Laura Sandelson
Editor: Lydia Darbyshire
Photographer: Paul Forrester

Typeset in Great Britain by
Central Southern Typesetters. Eastbourne
Manufactured in Hong Kong by
Regent Publishing Services Limited
Printed in China

ACKNOWLEDGEMENT
The publishers would like to thank
Dylon International Limited for supplying
the fabric paints used to make up the projects
for photography.

YKG. G / 0449965

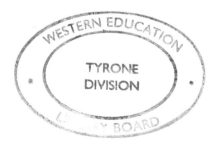

WESTERN EDUCATION
TYRONE
DIVISION
BOARD

Contents

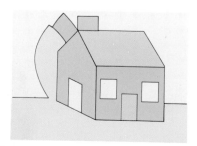

Introduction

Painting on fabric offers you the opportunity to create sensational effects on ordinary household items. Liven up a dull T-shirt or an old pair of jeans; design table linen to match your china, monogrammed bed linen, cushions to match your wallpaper and loads of other exciting things.

You don't have to be a great artist to master the art of fabric painting as many simple and effective designs can be done freehand. As your skills develop you can attempt more ambitious designs which require a steady hand, such as copying a motif from a book or magazine, or even making up your own design and transferring it onto fabric.

There are numerous ways of applying the paint to the fabric. Stencilling is an excellent way of covering a large area or creating a repeat pattern, for example on a tablecloth. Printing with sliced vegetables, fruit and flowers is a novel way of creating abstract patterns onto fabric — and it's dead easy: simply apply paint to the surface or edge of the object with which you are painting and print it directly onto the fabric. Throughout the book there are projects that incorporate masking, sponging, printing and painting on dark fabric so you become familiar with a whole range of fabric painting techniques.

Fabric paints come in many forms so you can create many different effects with puff, glitter and pearly paint. Colours can be easily mixed and applied to both natural and synthetic material. Furthermore, by ironing the newly-painted fabric on the wrong side, the article becomes colour-fast which means that it can be machine-washed time and time again. For best results new fabrics should be washed and ironed before paint is applied so that any dressing is removed which would prevent the paint from being absorbed. Remember to always place a piece of paper underneath the fabric onto which you are painting.

This book is specially designed for beginners: no expensive equipment is needed nor any special skills. Although suggestions have been given for colours and designs in all the projects there is no reason why you shouldn't try different combinations of colours and patterns. In many of the projects there are illustrations of alternative ways of painting the items to encourage you to use your imagination and, more importantly, to have fun with the paints.

Basic equipment you will need for painting on fabric.

Painted Espadrilles

Plain espadrilles come in a variety of bright colours, and they are inexpensive to buy. Decorating lighter colours — pale blue, green, pink and white — tends to be more successful than applying paint to darker shades. I have suggested using masking tape as a guide, but you may feel confident enough to apply the paint freehand.

You will need

◊ 1 pair of plain espadrilles
◊ Newspaper
◊ Masking tape
◊ Scissors
◊ Fabric paints (I used red, yellow and blue)
◊ Mixing palette
◊ Brushes (small and medium sizes)
◊ Tailor's chalk or coloured pencil)
◊ Iron
◊ Cloth

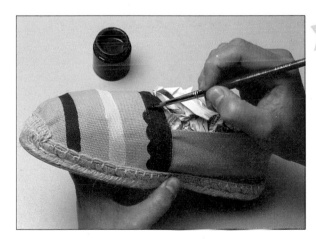

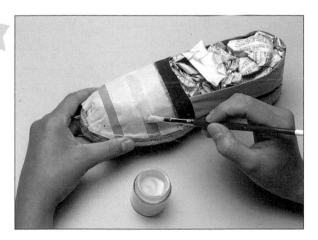

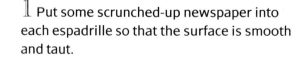

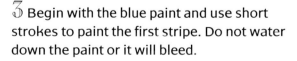

1 Put some scrunched-up newspaper into each espadrille so that the surface is smooth and taut.

2 Place three strips of masking tape across the front of the shoe, varying the distance between the pieces or using narrower tape if you want narrower or wider lines.

3 Begin with the blue paint and use short strokes to paint the first stripe. Do not water down the paint or it will bleed.

4 When you have painted the red and yellow stripes, leave the paint to dry before removing the masking tape.

5 Add the details to the stripes.

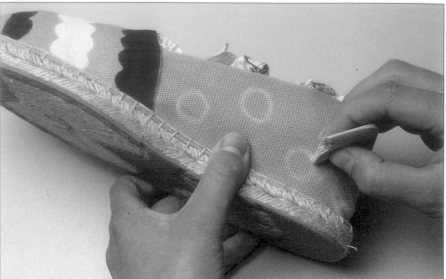

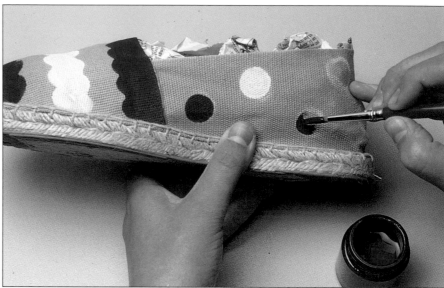

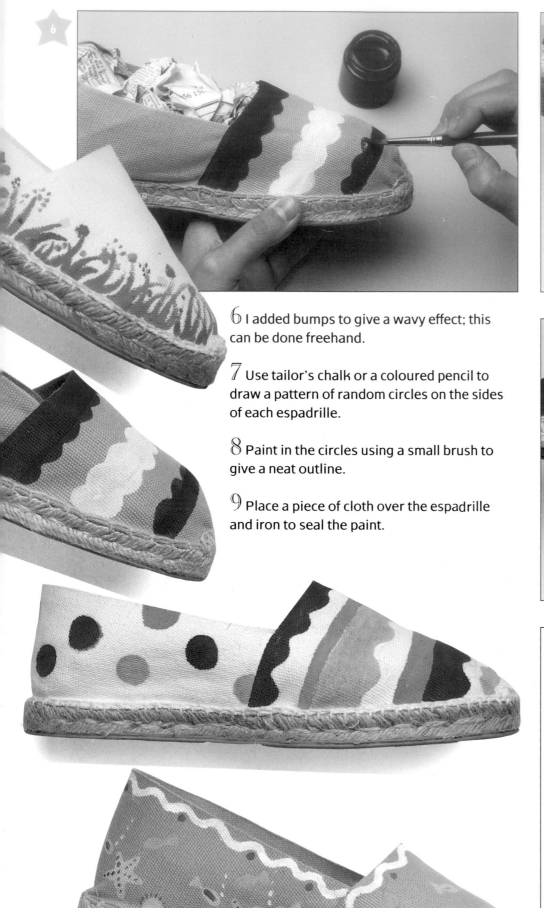

6 I added bumps to give a wavy effect; this can be done freehand.

7 Use tailor's chalk or a coloured pencil to draw a pattern of random circles on the sides of each espadrille.

8 Paint in the circles using a small brush to give a neat outline.

9 Place a piece of cloth over the espadrille and iron to seal the paint.

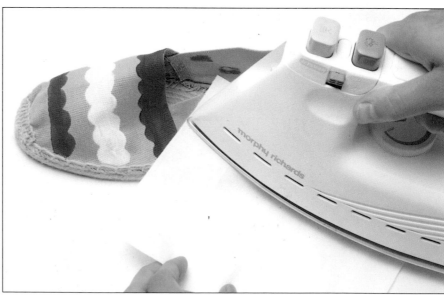

Customized Jeans

This project is an ideal way of experimenting with some of the more specialized fabric paints that are available these days — puff, glitter and fluorescent paints, for example. It is also a great way to liven up an old pair of jeans, and there are endless possibilities to try.

You will need
◊ Pair of jeans
◊ Newspaper
◊ Fabric paints (including puff, glitter and fluorescent)
◊ Mixing palette
◊ Paint brushes (various sizes)
◊ Hair-drier

1 Place a few sheets of newspaper inside the jeans to protect them from paint seeping through.

2 Use puff paint to draw zigzag lines around the pockets.

3 Add green dots to the inside of the zigzags.

4 Paint on a patch using a mixture of yellow and white. Draw on some cross-hatched squares using a mixture of blue and purple paint.

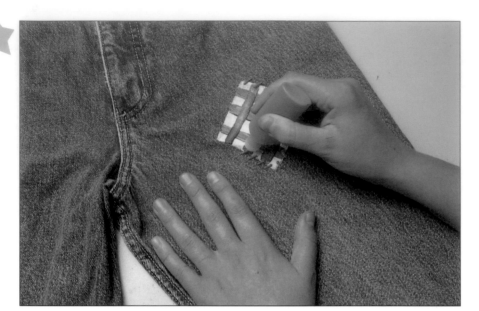

7 Add green puff paint crosses inside the heart and white dots around the edge. Add more patches down the legs of the jeans if you wish. When the paint is completely dry puff up the paint using a hair-drier.

5 Paint on "stitches" around the patch using pink puff paint.

6 Draw another motif on the other leg of the jeans — a pink heart, for example. Use green puff paint to draw a border around the heart.

Butterfly T-Shirt

Plain T-shirts in a wide range of colours and sizes are available all over the place, and if you buy them from a market they cost very little. Alternatively, you could give a new lease of life to an old T-shirt. I have drawn a butterfly design, but there is no limit to the patterns and motifs that you can try. This is an ideal project for experimenting with some of the specialized fabric paints, such as glitter paints, and puff paints, which change when they are exposed to the warmth of a hair-drier.

You will need
◊ Tracing paper
◊ Pencil
◊ Scissors
◊ Plain T-shirt
◊ Newspaper
◊ Pins
◊ Tailor's chalk or coloured pencil
◊ Fabric paints (including puff and glitter paints)
◊ Mixing palette
◊ Paintbrushes (various sizes)
◊ Hair-drier

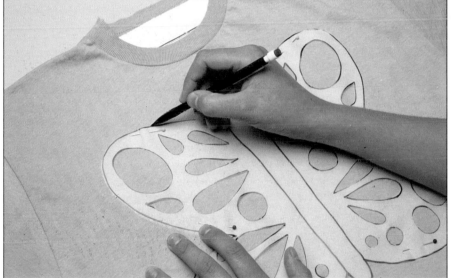

1 Trace the butterfly template from the outline on page 45 and cut it out. Cut out the holes in the wings.

2 Put newspaper inside the T-shirt to stop paint seeping through to the back. Pin the template to the front of the T-shirt and draw around the shape with a coloured pencil or tailor's chalk. Use a coloured pencil to add other details — the antennae, for example — freehand.

3 Paint in the wings using whatever colours you wish. Use a no. 6 paintbrush for the small dots and a ¼in/5mm brush for the larger ones.

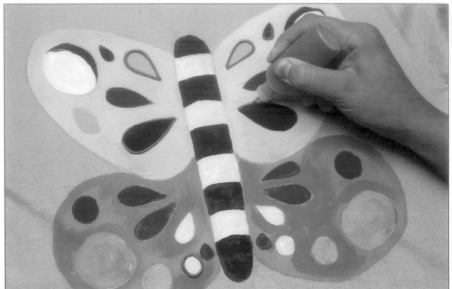

4 Add other colours. Allow the paint to dry for about 20 minutes before painting another colour next to it.

5 Add lines of puff paint around the patterns on the wings.

6 Add some spots of glitter paint around the neckline.

7 Outline the wing shapes in a different colour puff paint. Puff up the paint using a hair-drier.

Abstract Patterns

This is an ideal way of decorating lengths of plain fabric so that you can make them up into curtains, table linen, cushion covers or even clothes. Look around your home and you are sure to find countless bits and pieces — sponges, combs, jar lids, pen tops, pegs — that can be used to make interesting patterns. You could also experiment with food — pasta or potatoes, for example — to create some unusual designs.

You will need
◊ Items for printing — combs, cotton reels, pen tops, etc.
◊ Newspaper
◊ Fabric
◊ Masking tape
◊ Fabric paint
◊ Mixing palette
◊ Paintbrush (medium size)
◊ Iron
◊ Cloth

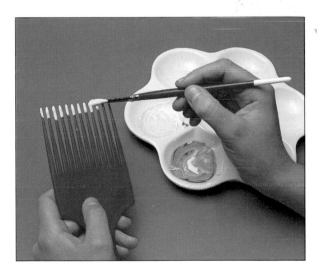

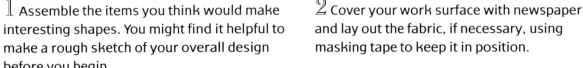

1 Assemble the items you think would make interesting shapes. You might find it helpful to make a rough sketch of your overall design before you begin.

2 Cover your work surface with newspaper and lay out the fabric, if necessary, using masking tape to keep it in position.

3 Mix the colours you want to use in a palette.

4 Apply paint to the object — I used a comb — taking care not to use too much paint or the outline will not look crisp and neat.

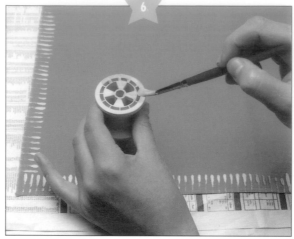

7 Incorporate the shape into your design. Leave to dry.

8 Use a different colour with your next object. I used a small piece of sponge, which gives an interesting and uneven texture.

9 Leave the third colour to dry before you apply the next series of coloured shapes. When you are satisfied with the pattern, iron under a cloth to fix the paints.

5 Use the comb to transfer the paint to the fabric. Continue all around the edge of the fabric, then leave to dry for about 20 minutes.

6 Take your next object – I used a wooden cotton reel – and paint the surface with a different colour.

Vegetable-printed Apron

Vegetables that have a distinctive shape, such as cabbage, mushrooms, chilies and broccoli, are ideal for fabric printing. Cut them in half and use them to decorate a plain calico apron of the kind you can buy in catering or do-it-yourself shops. Try experimenting with halved fruit.

You will need
◊ Selection of vegetables (broccoli, mushrooms, cabbage, okra, chili, etc.)
◊ Kitchen knife
◊ Pencil
◊ Plain paper
◊ Plain calico apron
◊ Newspaper
◊ Fabric paints
◊ Mixing palette
◊ Paintbrush (medium size)
◊ Fabric paint pens
◊ Iron
◊ Cloth

4 Test the cabbage on a piece of rough paper to check that the surface is smooth and gives an even impression. You will need to press fairly hard to get a good print, but do not put too much paint on the vegetable or the pattern will smudge.

1 Cut the vegetables you want to include in your design in half with a sharp knife. Include the stalks and cut more than one of each so that you can use several colours.

2 Draw a rough sketch on plain paper of how you want the apron to look.

3 Lay the apron on sheets of newspaper and prepare the paints. Use a paintbrush to paint the surface of, say, the cabbage.

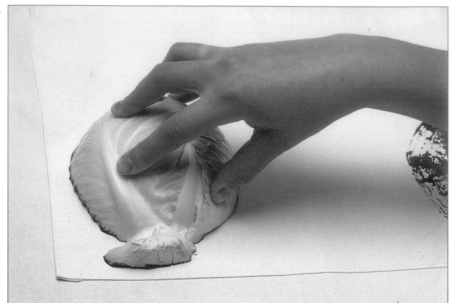

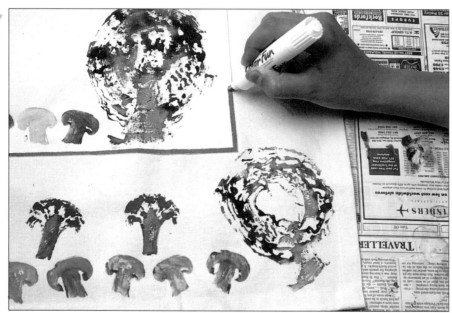

5 Print the cabbage on the apron.

6 Add more vegetable prints to build up your design, taking care not to move the vegetable as you apply pressure. Add fresh paint for every print.

7 Use a fabric marker pen to draw a line around the edge of the apron and to highlight the pocket edge. Iron under a cloth to fix the paints.

Printing with Flowers

This simple project uses flowers and leaves to decorate fabric, which could be used for cushion covers, table or bed linen or even curtains. Some kinds of plant material work better than others – flowers and leaves with sturdy, unfussy outlines give more successful prints than more delicate shapes. Try buddleia, ivy and conifer leaves and flowers such as daisies. The backs of leaves with prominent veins work especially well.

You will need
◊ Rough paper
◊ Coloured pencils
◊ Newspaper
◊ Fabric of your choice
◊ Masking tape
◊ A selection of flowers and leaves
◊ Fabric paints
◊ Mixing palette
◊ Paintbrush (medium size)
◊ Iron
◊ Cloth

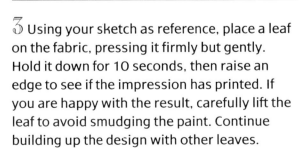

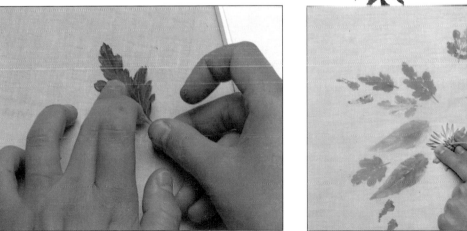

1 Position the flowers and leaves in a pleasing design. Make a rough sketch of the design and colour in the shapes so that you have a reference when you start to print.

2 Cover your work surface with newspaper and spread out your fabric, taping it in position if necessary. Mix your paints and paint some of the leaves.

3 Using your sketch as reference, place a leaf on the fabric, pressing it firmly but gently. Hold it down for 10 seconds, then raise an edge to see if the impression has printed. If you are happy with the result, carefully lift the leaf to avoid smudging the paint. Continue building up the design with other leaves.

4 Now paint a flower, placing it as indicated on your rough sketch. Fill in any gaps in the design and don't worry if some of the flowers look rather abstract. Leave to dry before ironing under a cloth to fix the paints.

Folk Art Picture

This charming image is achieved by applying a series of stencils, one after the other, and painting each in a different colour. You could frame the completed image, as I have done, or you could paint two and make up a pair of cushion covers.

You will need
◊ Tracing paper
◊ Pencil
◊ Stencil card
◊ Masking tape
◊ Craft knife or scalpel
◊ Piece of canvas or calico, approximately 13 × 11in/33 × 28cm
◊ Scissors
◊ Newspaper
◊ Stencil brush (¼in/5mm or ½in/12mm)
◊ Fabric paint
◊ Mixing palette
◊ Iron
◊ Cloth
◊ 4 buttons

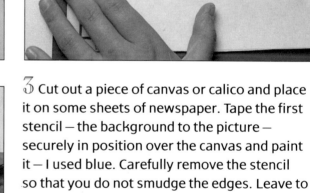

3 Cut out a piece of canvas or calico and place it on some sheets of newspaper. Tape the first stencil – the background to the picture – securely in position over the canvas and paint it – I used blue. Carefully remove the stencil so that you do not smudge the edges. Leave to dry for a few minutes.

4 Tape the second stencil – the house front and chimney piece – accurately in position and apply dark blue paint. Use a paintbrush to paint around the window areas.

1 Trace the stencil designs on pages 46 to 48, drawing each of the outlines onto equal sized sheets of paper so that they will all fit together accurately.

2 Tape each traced stencil onto a separate piece of stencil card, taking care to position each outline in the same position on each piece of card. Cut out the holes in each stencil.

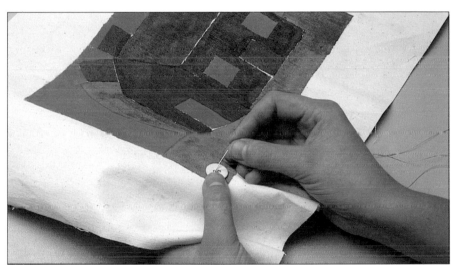

5 Leave the paint to dry before you use the next stencil.

6 Tape the next stencil – the front door and roof – in place. This time use brown paint. Again, leave to dry.

7 Tape the next stencil in place and then paint the side of the house purple. Leave to dry before using the last stencil, the foreground and trees, which are painted green.

8 Iron under a cloth to fix the paint and sew a button in each corner.

Child's Wall-hanging

This charming parade of stencilled animals would look great on a child's bedroom wall. The project uses simple, colourful hand-stitching and stencilling, which combine to give an old-fashioned, slightly folksy effect. You could make a similar piece using numbers or letters instead of animals.

You will need

◊ Tracing paper
◊ Pencils
◊ Stencil card
◊ Masking tape
◊ Craft knife or scalpel
◊ 8 pieces of cream-coloured fabric, each measuring approximately 5 × 5 in/12.5 × 12.5 cm
◊ Fabric paints
◊ Mixing palette
◊ Stencil brushes ¼ in/5mm and ½ in/12 mm
◊ Sponge (natural sponge is best)
◊ Iron
◊ Cloth
◊ 2 pieces of coloured fabric, each measuring approximately 50 × 8 in/128 × 20 cm (I used blue)
◊ Pins
◊ Scissors
◊ Needle
◊ Coloured embroidery silks
◊ 2 buttons
◊ Bias binding, tape or ribbon, approximately 4 in/10 cm

1 Trace the eight animal shapes from pages 44 and 45. Place each animal tracing on a piece of stencil card and hold it in place with masking tape.

2 Use a craft knife or scalpel to cut out each shape. Discard the tracing paper.

3 Cut out eight squares of cream-coloured fabric.

4 Use masking tape to hold each cut-out animal in position on a square of fabric.

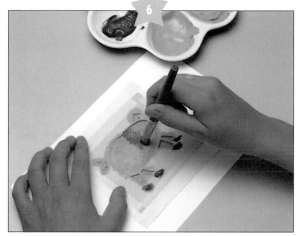

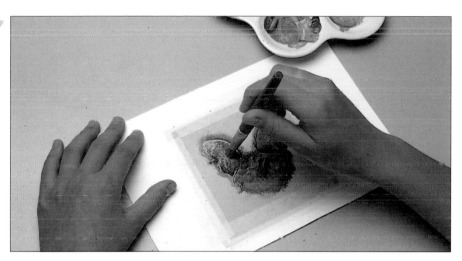

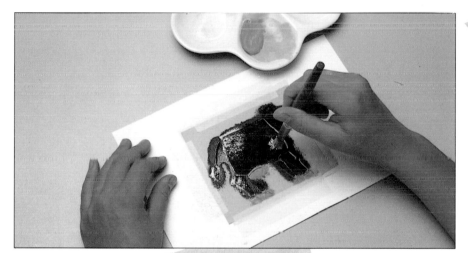

5 Prepare your paints, then colour the pig's body using a stencil brush.

6 Colour the pig's feet brown and add a band of brown across its body.

7 The cockerel has a blue-green body and a bright red comb.

8 Add some yellow and orange to the feathers in the cockerel's tail.

9 Colour the cow's body black and its hooves and udder pink. Make some spots by sponging on some white paint.

10 Paint the rest of the animals, using the photograph of the finished wall hanging as a guide. Turn under the edges of each square and iron under a cloth to fix the colours and press down the turned-back edges.

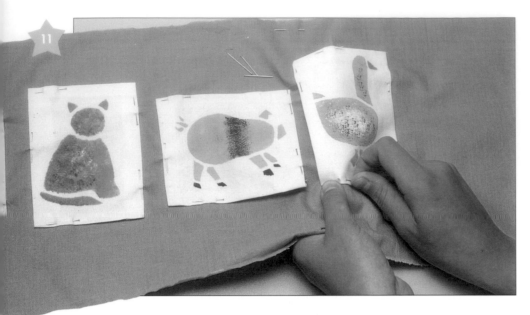

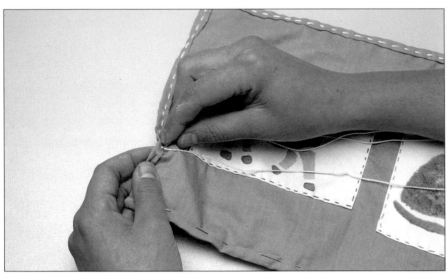

11 Place the two rectangles of fabric together and pin. Space the eight animal pictures evenly along one of the long rectangles of fabric, pinning them in position.

12 Use coloured embroidery silk and straight stitch to sew each square in place.

13 Turn the edge of the large rectangle into a neat hem on the front and hand sew with yellow embroidery silk.

14 Sew a button in each of the top corners and add loops of tape, bias binding or ribbon from which to hang it.

Marine Lampshade

Fabric paints can be used to decorate a plain lampshade to suit your own home furnishings. Plain, straight-sided lampshades are available in most do-it-yourself stores and large department stores, and they are not too expensive.
I have used simple sponging and stencilling techniques to create this peaceful underwater scene.

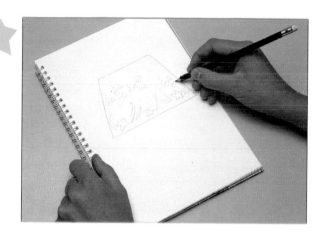

1 Sketch a rough plan of your ideas on plain paper before you begin.

2 Use a marker pen to draw the seaweed, fish and starfish shapes onto stencil card. If you prefer, draw the outlines in pencil first as a guide.

3 Use a craft knife or scalpel to cut out the shapes.

4 Cut the card into individual stencils.

5 Mix your colours and use an artist's sponge or a bath sponge cut into small pieces to start filling in the background of the design. Begin with a light layer of blue,

then add a second layer to make the tone darken gradually as it nears the top of the shade.

You will need
◊ Paper
◊ Pencil
◊ Marker pen
◊ Stencil card
◊ Craft knife or scalpel
◊ Scissors
◊ Plain lampshade
◊ Fabric paints
◊ Sponge (natural sponge is best)
◊ Masking tape
◊ Stencil brush ¼ in/5mm or ½ in/12mm

6 Add yellow around the bottom to represent sand. Leave to dry for about 20 minutes.

7 Tape the starfish stencil in position, referring to your sketch as a guide. Hold the lampshade firmly and use a stencil brush to colour the starfish red. Repeat until there is a series of starfish around the rim.

8 Tape the seaweed stencil in position and paint it green. Repeat the motif around the base but using different shades of green.

9 Next tape one of the fish stencils in place. Use different colours — I used blue, purple and red — and continue until there is a shoal of fish swimming all round the shade.

10 Paint in some air bubbles freehand.

Shopping Bag

The combination of the attractive fruit design and the durable nature of this simple canvas drawstring bag makes it the perfect way to carry heavy fruit and vegetables home from the market. Although I have supplied simple templates for the motifs, you could decorate it with an alternative pattern so that the bag could be used to carry school things or your sports kit.

1 Trace the fruit motifs from the templates on page 43 and cut out.

2 Cut two pieces of canvas. Place the templates on the canvas, pin them in position and use a pencil to draw around the outlines.

3 Use your traced outlines as a guide to fill in the details of the fruit.

4 Use a ruler to add the check tablecloth pattern.

5 Mix your paints. You will need yellow for the bananas, purple for the grapes (you can add some white, yellow and orange for a lighter shade of purple) and green for the apples.

You will need
◊ Tracing paper
◊ Pencil
◊ Scissors
◊ 2 pieces of canvas, each 18 × 16in/45.5 × 40.5cm
◊ Pins
◊ Ruler
◊ Fabric paint
◊ Mixing palette
◊ Paintbrushes (3 sizes)
◊ Fabric paint pen (blue)
◊ Iron
◊ Cloth
◊ Sewing machine
◊ Sewing thread
◊ ¼in/5mm cord, 30in/76.5cm long
◊ Safety pin

6 Use short strokes to apply the first colour. Aim to create a three-dimensional effect.

7 Paint the apples and bananas.

8 Colour the stalks and leaves of the apples.

9 Add the detail to the grapes, using dark green for the tendrils and brown for the stalks.

10 Add detail in brown to the bananas to make them look as natural as possible. Leave

the paint to dry for about 20 minutes, then iron under a cloth.

11 Paint in the white squares of the tablecloth border pattern and outline the squares with a blue fabric painting pen.

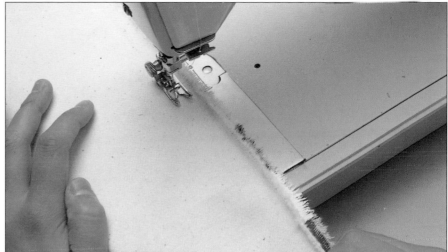

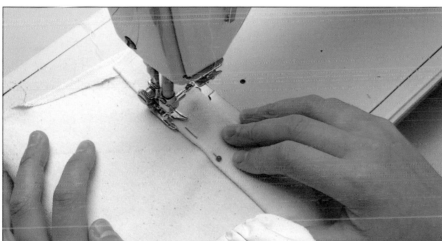

12 Colour in alternate squares and leave to dry for about 20 minutes. Iron under a cloth. Decorate the second piece of canvas in the same way if you wish.

13 With right sides together, sew one side of the bag with a sewing machine.

14 Open the bag so that the middle, inside seam faces you. On each side at the top, turn 2in/5cm of the raw edge inwards at an angle. Machine stitch into place. Fold back the bag with right sides together and machine stitch along the bottom and side. Turn right side out.

15 Use a safety pin to thread through the cord as a drawstring. Bind the ends of the cord to stop it from unravelling.

Napkins

These crisp, attractive napkins would be ideal for an outdoor meal or a summer dinner party. You could use the same motifs to decorate a matching tablecloth too, or you could devise your own motifs or colour schemes to decorate some napkins for Christmas, Easter or a themed birthday party.

You will need
◊ Tracing paper
◊ Pencil
◊ Scissors
◊ 4–6 squares of fabric, each measuring approximately 14 × 14in/35.5 × 35.5cm
◊ Pins
◊ Coloured pencil
◊ Ruler
◊ Tailor's chalk
◊ Fabric paints
◊ Mixing palette
◊ Paintbrushes (small and medium sizes)
◊ Iron
◊ Cloth
◊ Sewing machine
◊ Sewing thread

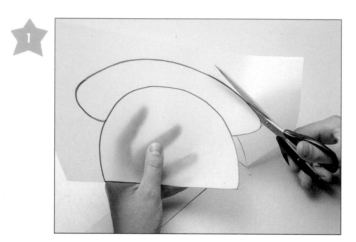

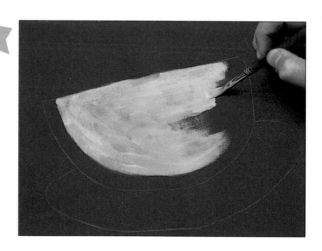

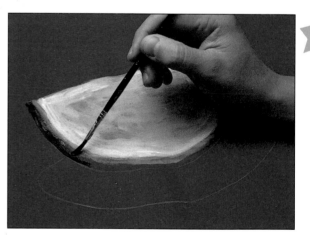

1 Draw freehand a watermelon slice on a plate and cut it out.

2 Cut out the squares of fabric and pin the watermelon illustration to one piece, placing it in the centre of the fabric. Use a coloured pencil – or, if your fabric is dark use a white pencil – and a ruler to draw the check border on the top and bottom edges of the square. The border should be about 1in/2.5cm wide.

3 Use tailor's chalk or a coloured pencil to draw around the template. Using a mixture of white and red, paint the flesh of the watermelon pink. Highlight the edges with white paint.

4 Paint the rind, first with light green then with a darker green.

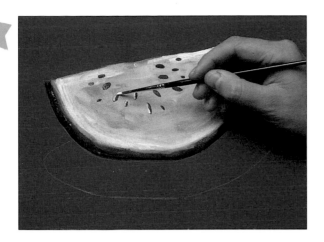

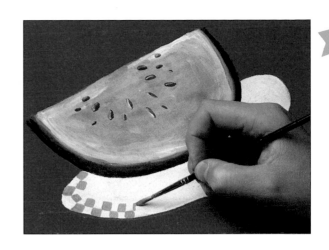

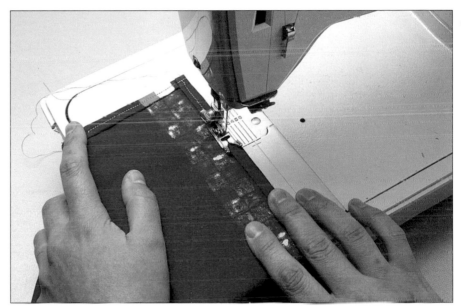

5 Add the pips with black paint, highlighting them with white.

6 Use white paint for the plate.

7 Add a blue-green check-pattern border to the plate, painting the squares freehand.

8 Paint alternate squares of the border with white and blue-green paint. Iron under a cloth to seal the colour.

9 Use a sewing machine to hem the edges.

Animal Cushions

Scatter these lively animal cushions on a child's bed or arrange them in a group on a chair. Watered-down fabric paints have been used to achieve the background colours, while thicker paints are used for the detailed markings. Simple embroidery stitches in brightly coloured threads have been added to enhance the details of feathers, whiskers and so on.

You will need
◊ Tracing paper
◊ Pencil
◊ Scissors
◊ Pins
◊ White cotton fabric, approximately 20 × 10in/51 × 25cm for each cushion
◊ Newspaper
◊ Fabric paints
◊ Mixing palette
◊ Paintbrushes (small and medium)
◊ Coloured embroidery silks
◊ Needle
◊ Sewing thread
◊ Sewing machine
◊ Kapok or other toy stuffing
◊ Buttons for eyes
◊ String for pig's tail

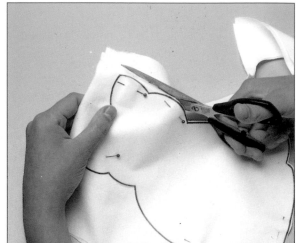

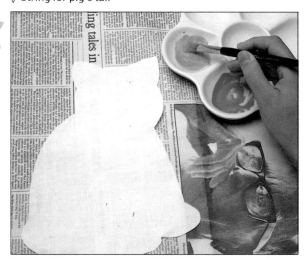

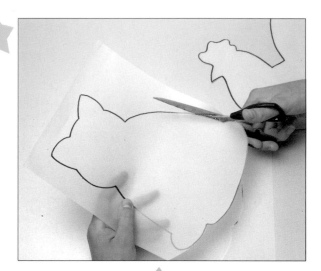

1 Trace the animal templates on pages 40 to 42 and cut out.

2 Pin each template to a double layer of fabric and cut around it.

3 Place each animal shape on some newspaper and prepare your paints.

4 Water down the paints that you are going to use for the background – for example, use orange for the cat – but do not make the

colour flat; it will look more natural if it is quite streaky.

5 Add spots on the back and head and a nose and tail, using the photograph on page 31 as a guide.

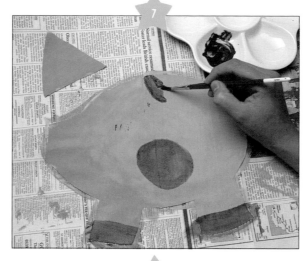

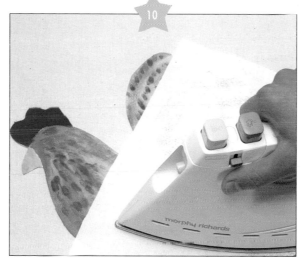

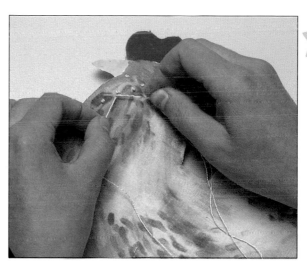

6 Make the pig in the same way and remember to include two ears.

7 Use brown paint for the pig's feet and the spots on its flanks.

8 The cockerel is more difficult. The background is a combination of green, purple, pink and yellow. Apply each colour separately but try to achieve a soft, feathery effect with no harsh edges to the colours.

9 Add a yellow beak and bright red comb.

10 Iron both sides of each of the animals under a cloth when you have finished them to seal the paints.

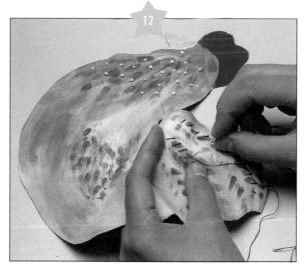

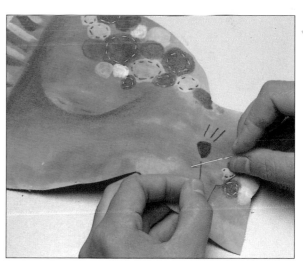

11 Use embroidery silks to stitch details on the cockerel's neck feathers.

12 Stitch some additional feather detailing to the cockerel's back.

13 Stitch around the spots on the cat and embroider the whiskers. Remember to stitch the cat's paws.

14 Pin the two pieces of the cushion together and use a sewing machine to stitch around the edge, leaving about 2in/5cm open along the bottom edge.

15 Carefully snip the curved edges up the stitching line so that the seams lie flat.

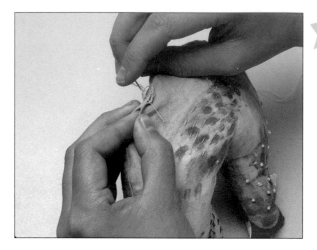

16 Turn the cushion to the right side, using the wrong end of a paintbrush to push out the seams, especially around the cockerel's beak and comb. Fill the cushion with Kapok or any soft toy stuffing material, pushing it into the head and tail with a piece of wooden dowel or the wrong end of a knitting needle.

17 Sew up the open seam. Repeat steps 14–17 for the pig and cat.

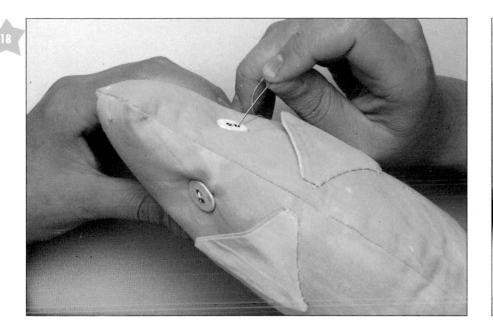

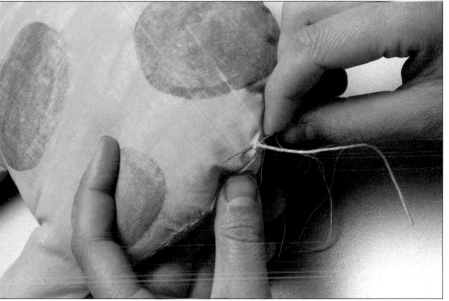

18 Stitch on buttons for eyes and remember to add the pig's ears.

19 Make a tail for the pig by painting some string pink and sewing it onto the pig's back.

Pillowcases

Simple stencilling techniques allow you to decorate plain cotton pillowcases with a fresh floral design, and once you have mastered the techniques there is no need to stop at pillowcases: you can decorate a duvet cover and sheet to match. I have supplied templates for the flowers, but you may prefer to design your own motifs.

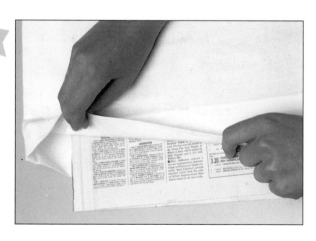

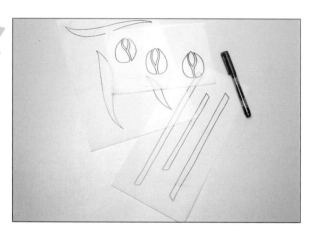

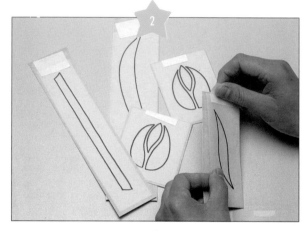

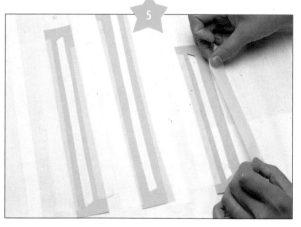

You will need
◊ Marker pen
◊ Tracing paper
◊ Masking tape
◊ Stencil card
◊ Craft knife or scalpel
◊ 2 plain cotton pillowcases
◊ Newspaper
◊ Fabric paint
◊ Mixing palette
◊ Stencil brush
◊ Iron
◊ Cloth

1 Use a marker pen to trace the stencil patterns from the outlines on page 38.

2 Use masking tape to hold the traced shapes securely in position on the stencil card.

3 Cut around the shapes with a craft knife or scalpel, working on a cutting mat or a piece of thick cardboard. Discard the tracing paper.

4 Put some pieces of newspaper inside the pillowcase to protect the other side from any paint that seeps through.

5 Position the stem templates on the pillowcase, securing them with masking tape.

6 Mix the paint colours. Paint in the stems with a small (¼in/5mm) stencil brush and use different shades of green.

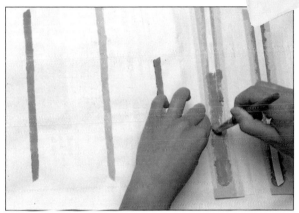

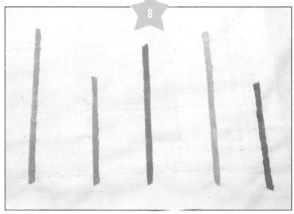

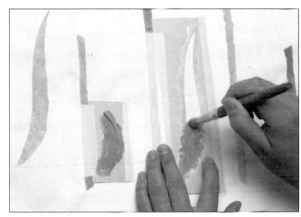

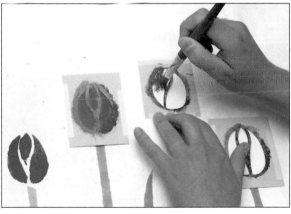

7 Dab rather than use brush strokes for a "sponging" effect and take care not to splash the paint onto the rest of the pillowcase.

8 Repeat until there are stems across the pillowcase – about eight in all. Remove the stencils.

9 Position the leaf stencils and secure them with masking tape. Colour the leaves as you did the stems, holding the stencil firmly down with your fingers so that paint does not bleed under the cut edge.

10 Position the flower stencils and hold them in place with masking tape. You could paint them all the same colour or in various shades of red – add orange, yellow or purple, for example.

11 Allow the paint to dry, then iron with a piece of cloth over the paint to fix the colours.

Doll

This simple doll makes a delightful gift for a child older than five or six years of age. You could design a different outfit if you preferred, or you could base the doll's appearance on someone you know. If you wish you could add extra details such as a hair ribbon, a hat or a piece of jewellery.

You will need
◊ Sketch pad
◊ Coloured pencils
◊ Tracing paper
◊ Pencil
◊ Piece of white fabric, 13 × 10in/33 × 25cm
◊ Pins
◊ Scissors
◊ Newspapers
◊ Kapok or other toy stuffing
◊ Sewing machine
◊ Sewing thread
◊ Fabric paints
◊ Mixing palette
◊ Paintbrushes (various sizes)
◊ Iron
◊ Cloth
◊ Needle
◊ Buttons

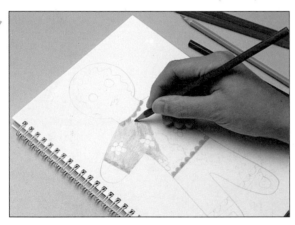

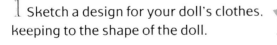

1 Sketch a design for your doll's clothes, keeping to the shape of the doll.

2 Trace the doll's template from page 39 and cut out. Fold the white fabric in half (so that it measures 13 × 5in/33 × 12.5cm) and pin the template to it, making sure that the pins go through both layers. Cut out the outline, adding a seam allowance of ⅛in/3mm all round.

3 Using your sketch as a reference, pencil guidelines on the cut-out doll – hairline, top, trousers, shoes and so on. Add the details to front and back.

4 Cover your work surface with newspaper and paint the front of the doll. Begin with the background colour of the blouse – I used blue.

5 Next paint in the shoes and trousers and then the mouth, cheeks and hair.

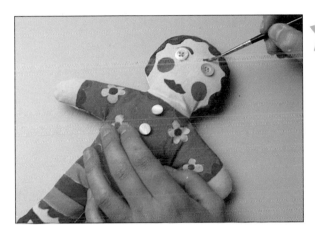

6 Allow the paint to dry, then add details such as the flower pattern to the top and the frills around the neck and trousers.

7 Paint the face pale pink and leave to dry. Paint the back of the doll to match. Iron.

8 Place the two pieces, right sides together, and machine stitch all the way around the doll, leaving a gap of about 2in/5cm under one arm. Carefully snip into the curves, up to the sewing line, at the neck, between the legs and at the ends of the arms and legs so that the seams lie smoothly.

9 Turn the doll the right way out. You may find it helpful to use the wrong end of a paintbrush to push the arms and legs through. Fill the doll with Kapok or any other soft toy stuffing, adding little pinches at a time and using a piece of wooden dowel or the wrong end of a knitting needle to push the filler down into the arms and legs. Stitch up the underarm seam opening.

10 Sew on buttons for the eyes.

11 Paint on the eyebrows.

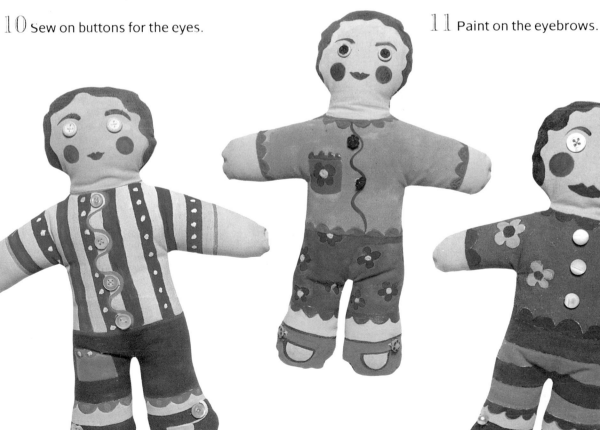

Herb Sachet

Scented sachets make ideal gifts. They can be hung among clothes in a wardrobe or placed in drawers where they will delicately perfume your clothes. I have shown how to paint a very simple design, but you may feel ambitious enough to attempt a more detailed and realistic floral pattern using several colours.

You will need
◊ Piece of white cotton, approximately
   8½ × 6in/21.5 × 15cm
◊ Piece of pale-coloured cotton,
   3½ × 3in/9 × 7.5cm (I used green)
◊ Scissors
◊ Pencil
◊ Fabric paint
◊ Mixing palette
◊ 2 brushes (small)
◊ Iron
◊ Cloth
◊ Pins
◊ Sewing thread
◊ Sewing machine
◊ Lace trim, approximately 8½in/12.5cm
   long
◊ Scissors
◊ 2 buttons
◊ ¼in/5mm ribbon, approximately
   10in/25cm long
◊ Dried lavender

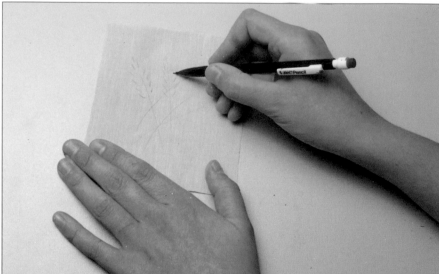

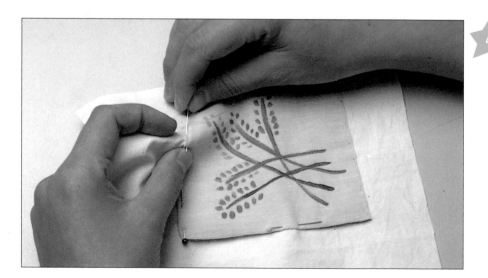

1 Cut out the pieces of white and coloured fabrics and put the white material to one side.

2 Draw the lavender flower pattern on the coloured fabric.

3 Paint in the outlines you have drawn, allow the paint to dry, then iron the painted pattern under a cloth.

4 Place the painted square at one end of the white cotton rectangle. Turn each edge neatly under approximately ¼in/5mm; pin and baste into position.

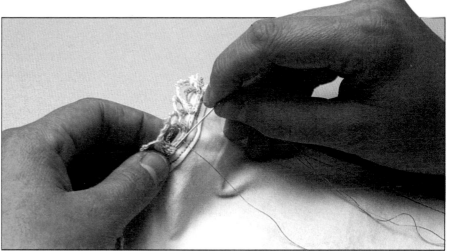

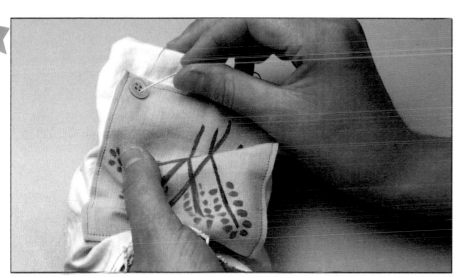

5 Use a sewing machine to stitch the square into position.

6 Turn over the top edge of the rectangle, pin, baste and machine stitch into position. Fold the rectangle in two, with the painted piece on the inside and with the short ends together. Sew along the bottom and along the open short edge. Stitch on the lace trim by hand. Turn to the right side.

7 Sew the buttons on the front.

8 Catch the ribbon in position with a stitch or two at the side seam, fill the sachet with dried lavender and tie the bow firmly.

Templates

PILLOWCASES

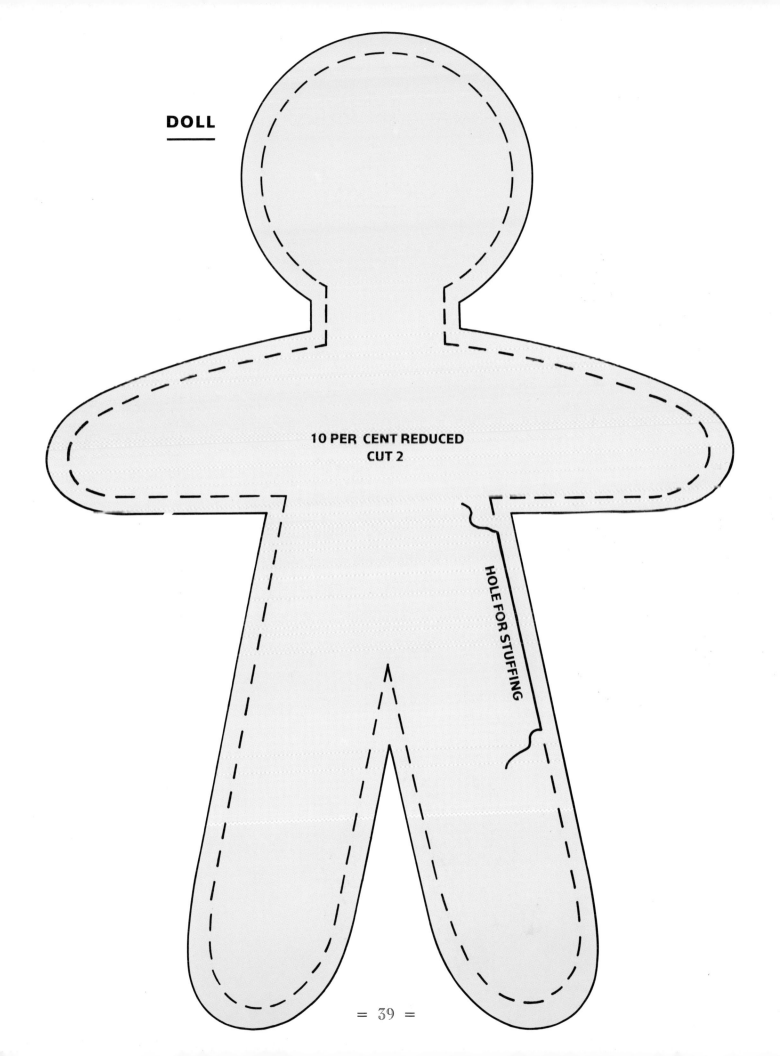

DOLL

10 PER CENT REDUCED
CUT 2

HOLE FOR STUFFING

ANIMAL CUSHIONS

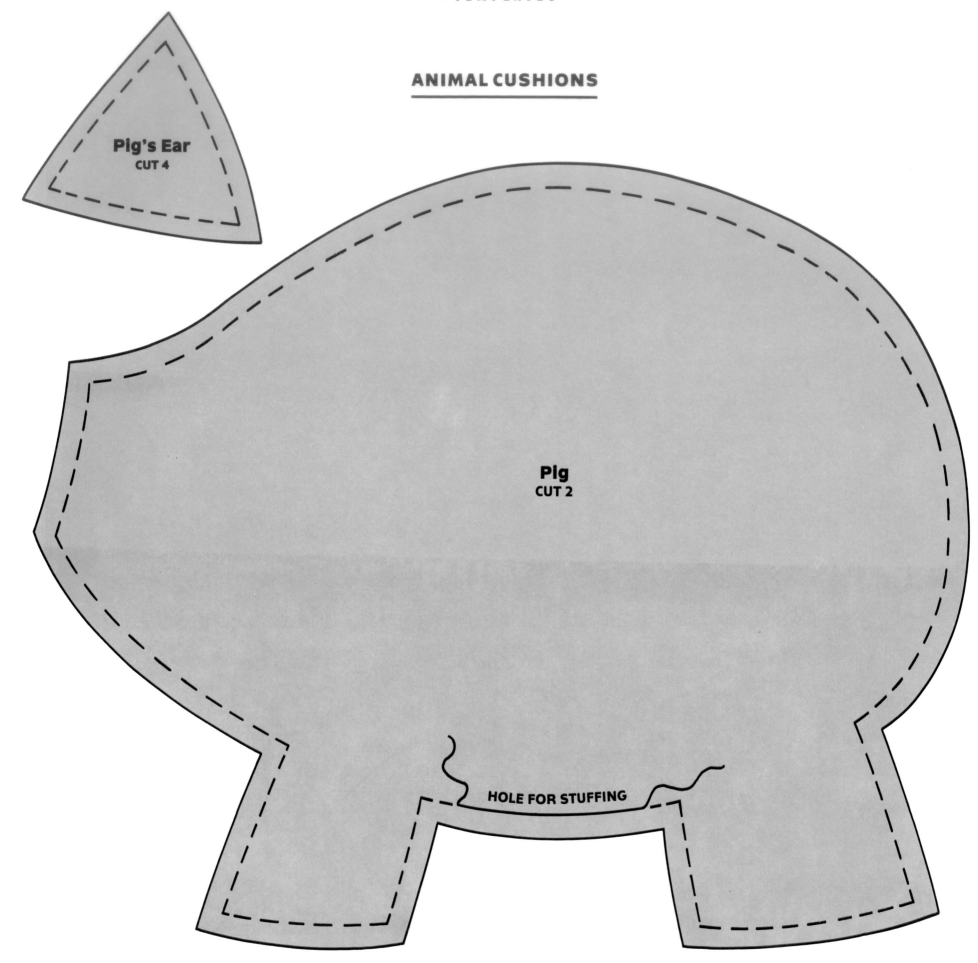

Pig's Ear
CUT 4

Pig
CUT 2

HOLE FOR STUFFING

ANIMAL CUSHIONS

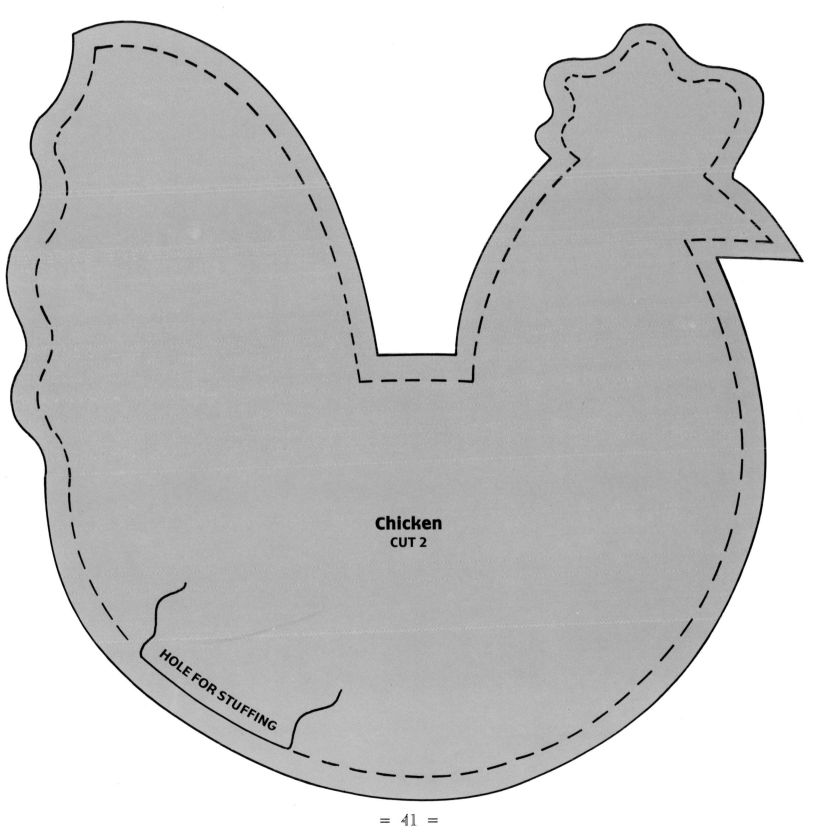

Chicken
CUT 2

HOLE FOR STUFFING

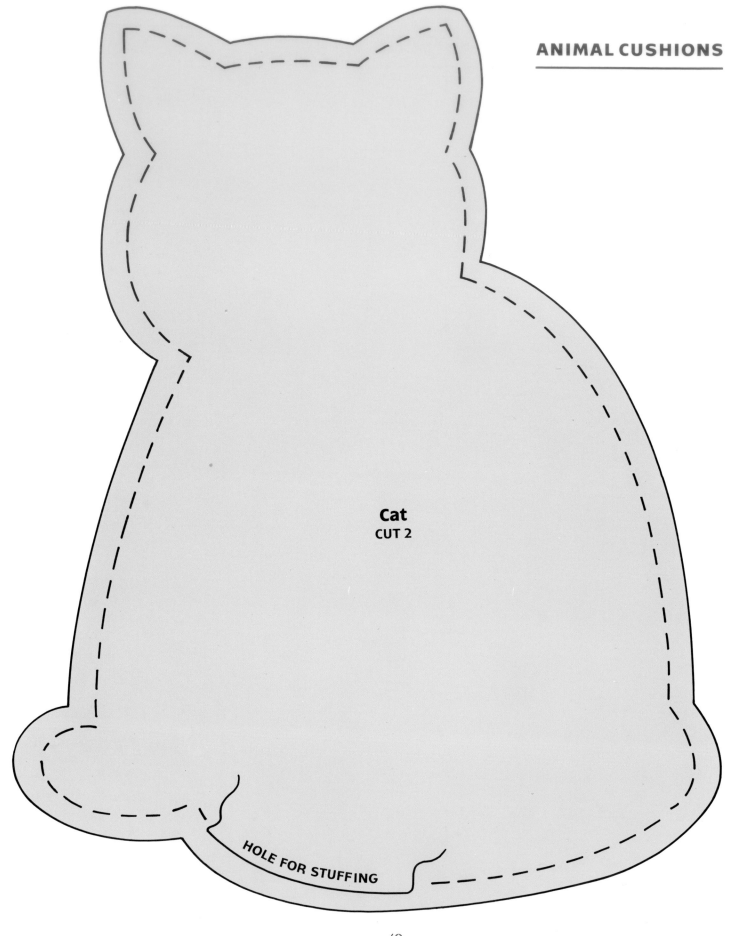

ANIMAL CUSHIONS

Cat
CUT 2

HOLE FOR STUFFING

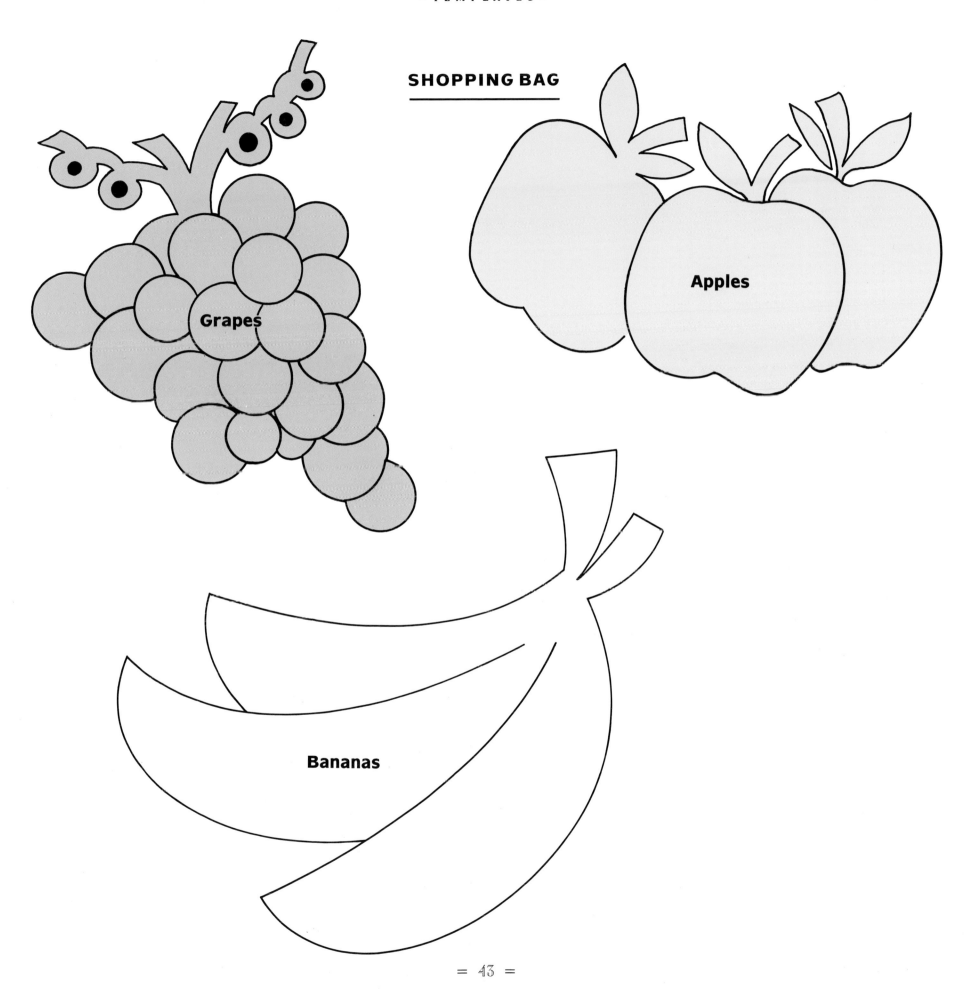

SHOPPING BAG

Grapes

Apples

Bananas

ANIMAL WALL HANGING

Horse

Goose

Cat

Pig

Dog

Sheep

**BUTTERFLY
T-SHIRT**

Chicken

Cow

FOLK ART PICTURE

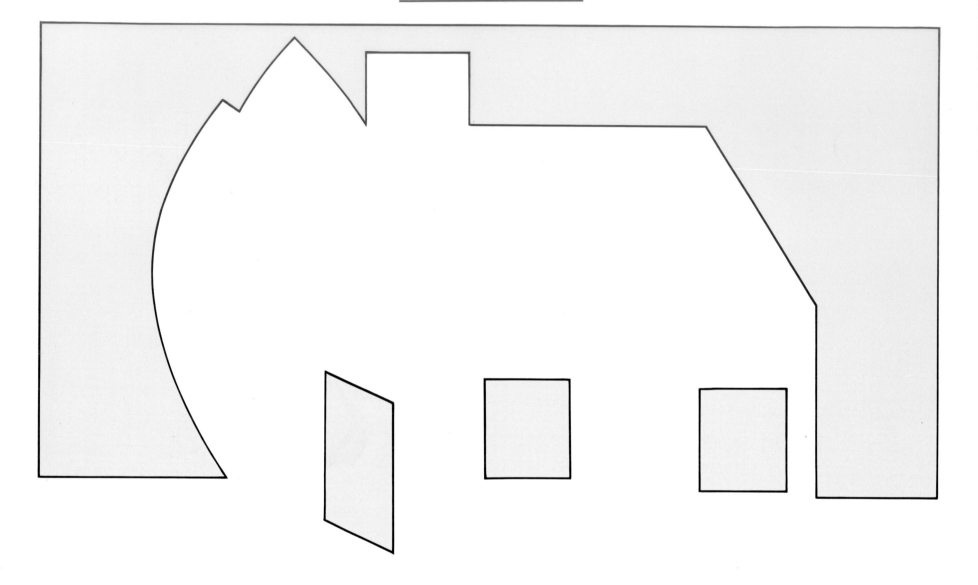

FOLK ART PICTURE

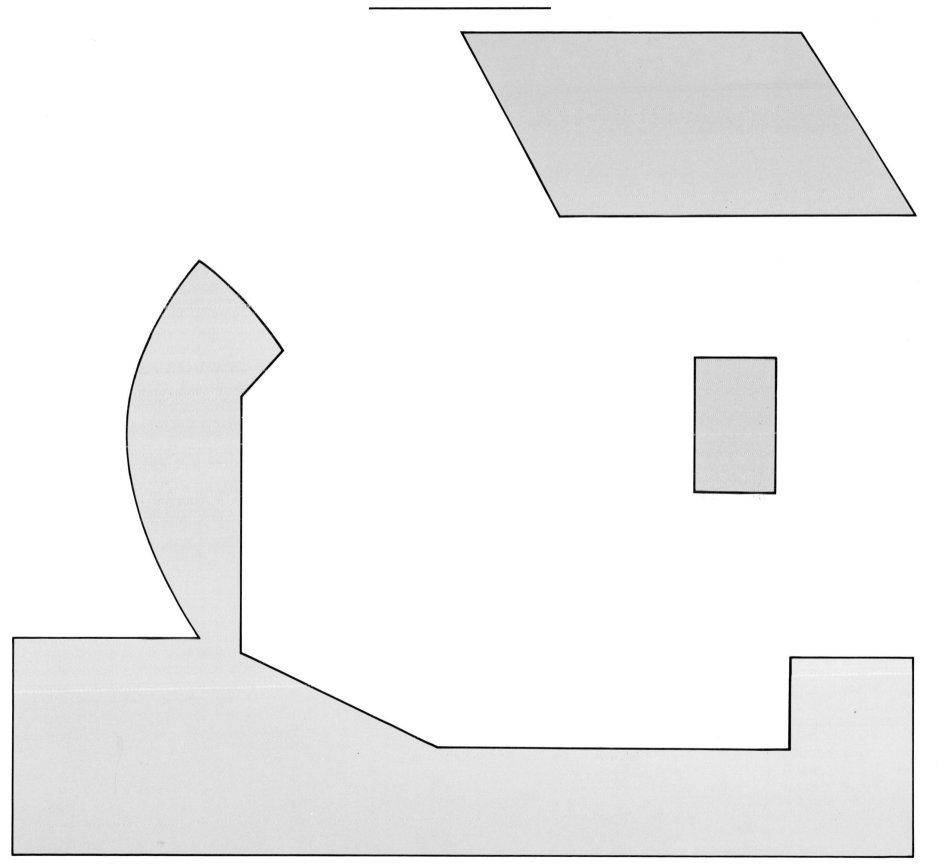

FOLK ART PICTURE

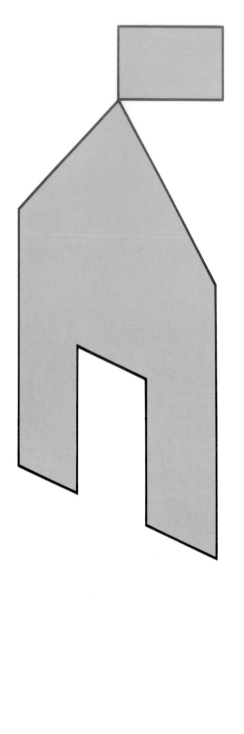

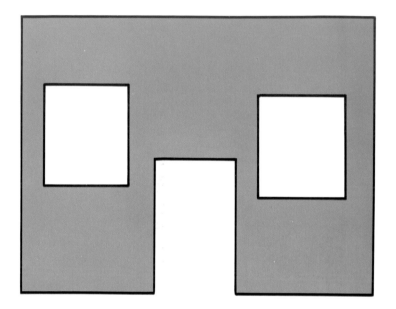

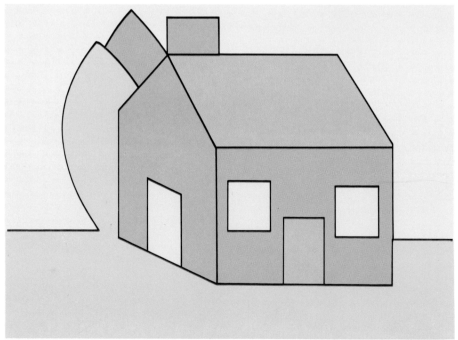

STENCILS IN PLACE